50
Rainy Day
Activities

Contents

Foil fish

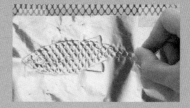

1. Use a ballpoint pen to draw a fish on the shiny side of a piece of kitchen foil. Then, tape the foil onto a net vegetable bag.

2. Use your thumbnail to gently rub the foil, inside the outline of the fish. This will make the net pattern appear on the foil.

3. Draw a green stripe on the fish's back with a felt-tip pen. Add a light green stripe, then fill in the rest of the fish with a yellow pen.

4. Draw purple and orange lines on the head. Add an eye with a black felt-tip pen. Make more fish, then cut them all out.

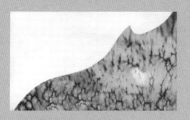

5. Cut a wavy line across a sheet of dark blue textured paper for the sea. Then, stick it onto a piece of light blue paper, like this.

6. Spread white glue on the back of each fish and press them firmly onto the blue background. Make some of them overlap the edge.

Princess hat

1. Draw half a circle on a large sheet of thick paper and cut it out. Bend the paper around and pinch the middle of the straight edge.

2. Wrap the curved edge of the half circle around your head. Ask someone to slide one edge over the other until the cone fits neatly.

Overlap the pieces of tissue paper as you glue them on.

3. While the cone is on your head, get someone to tape it together for you. Tape it on the outside, and then on the inside, too.

4. Rip different shades of tissue paper into small pieces. Brush glue over one patch of the cone at a time and press the pieces onto it.

5. Cover the whole cone in the same way. Then, cut several long strips of tissue paper or crêpe paper and tape them to the top.

6. Cut two hearts from shiny paper. Then, glue them onto the top of the cone, to hide the tape. Decorate your hat with sequins or stickers.

Flower garland

1. Lay a saucer on a piece of pale pink paper and use a pencil to draw around it. Then, draw around a mug on a piece of bright pink paper.

2. Draw around a bottle top on a piece of white paper. Then, cut out all the circles you have drawn and glue them together, like this.

3. For the petals, cut very thin triangles into the biggest circle. Only cut as far as the edge of the bright pink circle.

4. Make more flowers. Then cut a drinking straw into short pieces. Tape one piece of straw near the top of each flower, like this.

5. With the pieces of straw at the tops of the flowers, thread a long piece of ribbon through them all. Then, hang the flowers up.

Cut-paper card

1. For the card, use scissors to cut a large rectangle from thick white paper. Then, fold the rectangle in half, like this.

2. Cut four squares roughly the same size as each other from thick bright paper. Then, glue the squares onto the folded card.

3. Cut a leaf shape from green paper and glue it onto one of the squares. Then, cut thin veins and a long stem and glue them on.

4. Draw a flower and cut it out. Then, cut out a middle, a stalk and a leaf. Glue all the pieces onto one of the other squares.

5. Cut a strawberry shape from pink paper and glue it on another square. Cut out a stalk and small triangles and glue them on, too.

6. Cut a heart from bright paper and glue it onto the last square. Then, cut a smaller heart from patterned paper and glue it on top.

Chalk ballerina

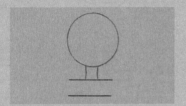

Use yellow and white chalks.

1. Draw a circle for the head at the top of a piece of blue paper. Add two short lines for her neck. Then, draw two lines for her shoulders.

2. Use a chalk pastel or a piece of chalk to draw the bodice of her dress. Then, draw lots of long zigzag lines beneath it for the skirt.

Paint across her shoulders, too.

3. Mix some paint for her skin using red, yellow, white and a tiny amount of blue paint. Fill in her face and neck, then paint her arms.

4. Paint legs coming from beneath her skirt. Then, add the feet. If your ballerina is pointing her toes, then paint a straight leg, with no foot.

5. When the paint has dried, use chalk to draw her hair. Add ribbons in her hair and on her shoulders. Draw her face with pens or pencils.

6. Use the chalk to draw her ballet shoes. Add crossed lines around her ankles and add tiny bows. Then, draw a ribbon around her waist.

Speckled butterflies

1. Paint all over a sheet of thick white paper with watery paint. Then, sprinkle grains of salt onto the paint and leave it to dry.

2. When the paint is dry, brush off the salt. Then, fold the paper in half and glue it together with the paint on the outside.

The fold needs to be on this side.

3. Fold the paper in half again. Draw two butterfly wings on it, then cut around the wings, through all the layers of paper.

4. For each butterfly, cut the end off a drinking straw, just above the bumpy part. To make feelers, cut down into the bumpy part.

Snip here.

Make sure that the bead is wider than the straw.

5. Bend the feelers out, then open the wings. Lay the straw in the fold in the middle, then snip off the bottom end of the straw.

6. Push a piece of ribbon through a bead. Tie a knot in the ribbon and push it through the straw. Glue the straw onto the wings.

19

Bird patterns

1. Using scissors, cut a corner off a square of thin cardboard. Then, tape the triangle along the top edge of the square, like this.

2. Cut the other corner off the bottom of the square. Tape it along the top, so that the two triangles meet in the middle.

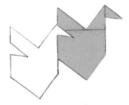

3. To make the bird's beak, cut a long 'v' shape into the left-hand side. Then, tape the shape onto the triangle on the right.

4. Draw around the bird shape. Then, move it so that the beak of the outline fits under the wing. Draw around it again.

5. Draw around the shape lots more times, to build up a pattern of birds, like this. The birds should fit into each other on all sides.

6. Paint the birds in three different shades, then let the paint dry. Use a black felt-tip pen to outline the birds, then add eyes, too.

Flower collage

1. Rip some long strips of blue tissue paper. Glue them across a piece of paper, so that they overlap.

2. Cut some thin strips of green tissue paper for stems and glue them along the bottom of the paper.

3. Cut out lots of rounded petals from red tissue paper. Glue four petals at the top of some of the stems.

4. Cut out orange petals, too. Glue them at the top of other stems, so that some overlap the red petals.

5. Use a thin black felt-tip pen to draw around each petal. You don't need to follow the edges exactly.

6. Draw a small circle in the middle of each flower, then add two or three lines on each petal.

Party mask

1. Cut long strips from pink and blue tissue paper. Make them the width of two fingers.

2. Glue the blue strips across a piece of cardboard. Glue the pink strips going the other way.

3. Turn over the cardboard. Lay a pair of sunglasses on it and draw around them.

4. Draw shapes where your eyes will be. Add a mask shape around the outline. Cut it out.

5. Press a sharp pencil point, then a scissor blade into the eyeholes. Cut out the eyeholes.

6. Turn the mask over. Draw lines of glitter glue along the edges of the tissue paper strips.

7. Cut a strip of shiny paper, big enough to cover a straw. Spread glue on the back of it.

Don't cover the bumpy part.

8. Lay the long end of a bendable straw at the edge of the paper. Roll the straw in the paper.

Tape over the bumpy part to make it stronger.

9. Trim the ends of the paper. Bend the straw. Then, tape the short part to the back of the mask.

Fairy puppet

This side of the wing needs to be on the fold.

1. Fold a piece of thick paper in half and draw a wing shape on it, like this. Then, keeping the paper folded, cut out the shape.

2. Open out the wings and flatten them. Then, draw a shape for the fairy's body and arms on bright paper. Cut out the shape.

3. Cut a paper circle for the head and a shape for the hair. Glue the hair onto the head and draw the face with a black felt-tip pen.

4. Cut out two hands from paper and glue them onto the back of the fairy's arms. Then, glue the head onto the body.

Decorate the fairy with pens and stickers.

5. Glue the body onto the wings, then decorate the fairy. Turn her over and tape a drinking straw onto the back of her body.

Mermaid bookmark

1. Fold a piece of foil in half. Then, spread a thin layer of white glue on the inside and press the foil together. Leave the glue to dry.

2. Put the foil on a pile of newspapers. Pressing hard with a ballpoint pen, draw a crown and a mermaid's tail. Then, cut out the shapes.

3. Lay the crown on the sticky side of some book covering film. Sprinkle a little glitter around it, then lay tissue paper over the top.

Cut a shape for her face in the hair.

4. Draw a wavy shape for the hair on the tissue paper. Cut out the hair and glue it onto the bumpy side of the tail, like this.

You could draw a fan-shaped or bumpy tail.

5. Glue the tail and the hair onto a piece of paper. Draw the mermaid's face and arms on the paper, then cut around the shapes.

Elephant chain

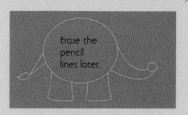

1. Using a pencil, lightly draw an oval for an elephant's body on thick paper. Draw two leg shapes below the body, too.

2. Draw a thick trunk with a circle at the end. For the tail, draw a thin triangle with a tassel at the end. Then, cut out the elephant.

They should all face the same way.

3. Draw around the elephant on different shades of paper, then cut out the elephants. Draw eyes and ears in black felt-tip pen.

4. Cut out shapes for the elephants' tusks and toenails from shiny paper or foil. Then, glue them onto the elephants.

Use a very small piece of tape.

5. Decorate the elephants by cutting out different shapes and gluing them on. Use sequins, beads, pens and glitter glue, too.

6. Make a small cut into each elephant's trunk. Slot the thin part of another elephant's tail into the slit. Secure them all with tape.

Matchbox trick

For this trick, you will need:
An empty matchbox
A pencil
A used match
A pair of scissors
String

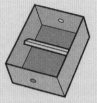

1. Take the tray out of an empty matchbox. Then, use a sharp pencil to make a small hole at each end of the tray, like this.

2. Trim a used match with scissors to make it just bigger than the width of the tray. Then, wedge it across the inside of the tray.

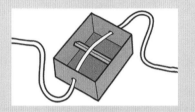

3. Thread a long piece of string through the holes in the tray and over the match. Then, push the tray back into the box.

4. Push the matchbox near one end of the string. Pull the string to stretch it tight, then hold it vertically with the box at the top.

5. Tell the audience that you can control the matchbox. Ask a volunteer from the audience to command the matchbox to "go" and "stop".

6. Relax the string to make the matchbox move. Then, to stop it, stretch the string tight. Make it move at the volunteer's command.

Paper caterpillar

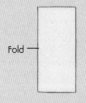

Fold ——

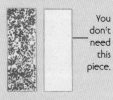

You don't need this piece.

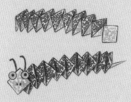

1. Fold a piece of bright paper in half, with the long sides together. Then, cut along the fold.

2. Sponge a different shade of bright paint on each side of one of the pieces of paper.

3. Fold the paper in half, then in half again. Open it and cut along the folds to make four strips.

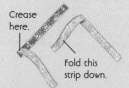

Crease here.

Fold this strip down.

4. Dab some glue at the end of one strip. Then, press on the end of another strip, like this.

5. Fold the left strip over and crease the fold. Then, fold the other strip down over it.

6. Keep folding one strip neatly over the other one, until you have made a zigzag shape.

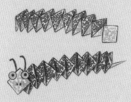

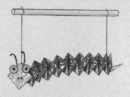

7. When you get to the end of the strips, glue on the spare strips and fold them to the end.

8. Glue down the ends, then glue on eyes and a tail. Add short feelers cut from a pipe cleaner.

9. Tape a piece of thread behind the head and the tail. Then, tie the ends onto a straw.

Flower bracelet

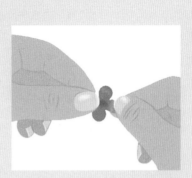

1. Cut a long piece of narrow ribbon that goes once around your wrist, with a little extra for tying on the bracelet.

2. Draw three hearts and two flowers on pieces of bright paper. Cut them out, then bend the petals with your fingers, like this.

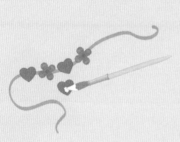

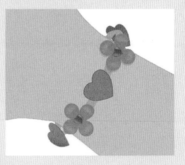

3. Using white glue, glue one heart onto the middle of the ribbon. Glue a flower on either side, then glue on the other hearts, too.

4. Glue a sequin in the middle of each flower. Then, when the glue is dry, ask someone to tie the bracelet around your wrist.

Pirate flags

1. To make the flags, fold several narrow rectangles of paper in half, with their short ends together. Crease the folds well.

2. With the fold at the top, draw an upside down 'V' at the bottom of each flag. Then, cut along the lines, keeping the layers together.

The glue stops the flags from sliding along the thread.

3. Draw skulls and bones, anchors, flags and palm trees on pieces of paper. Cut out the shapes and glue them onto the flags.

4. Open out the flags and spread glue along the folds. Fold the flags over a long piece of thread and press the glued parts together.

Daisy chains

1. Fold a rectangle of white paper in half, with its short edges together. Then, fold the paper in half again.

2. Draw a daisy near the top of the paper. Add a thick stem on each side. Then, draw two more daisies below.

Make all the stems go off the sides of the paper.

3. Using scissors, cut around all the daisies, but don't cut along the folds at the ends of the stems.

4. Open out the daisy chains. Then, use a yellow felt-tip pen to add the middles of the daisies.

Draw the edges of the petals first.

5. Fill in the stems with a green felt-tip pen. Then, tape the chains together to make one long chain.

Patterned birds

1. Draw two squares on a piece of brown giftwrap. Then, use a pencil to draw a simple outline of a bird in each square, like this.

2. Paint one bird pink and the other black. Then, paint the squares black and blue. Don't worry if a little of the paper shows through the paint.

3. When the paint is completely dry, draw a square around the pink bird with blue chalk pastels. Then, add some patterns.

4. Add legs and feet, and outline the body with a pale chalk pastel. Then, use a bright pastel to add lines on the bird and in the square.

5. Use a dip pen and black ink, or a black felt-tip pen, to add an eye, beak and lines on the body. Paint some black spots, too.

6. Draw legs and feet on the black bird with a black pastel. Using blue and green pastels, add an eye and lots of lines and patterns.

Paper fairy cake

Make each layer smaller than the one below.

1. Cut a rectangle of tissue paper for the bottom layer of a cake. Glue it onto some paper. Then, cut more layers and glue them on, too.

2. Use a thin black felt-tip pen to draw around each layer. Decorate the layers with patterns, such as circles, hearts and wavy lines.

Add more hearts and spots with the gold pen.

3. Draw holders for candles on some of the layers. Then, cut candles from tissue paper and glue them on. Add flames with a gold pen.

4. Cut a shape from tissue paper for a fairy's dress. Glue it near the cake. Cut two pairs of wings and glue them next to the dress.

Draw a wavy line along the bottom of the dress.

Fill in the wand, too.

5. Use a black pen to draw around the dress and the wings. Draw a neck and a curve for the chin. Then, add arms and legs.

6. Draw the fairy's hair with a gold pen. Then, draw her face and add a wand. Decorate her dress and legs with the gold pen.

Printed ghosts

1. Glue a sponge cloth onto a piece of thin cardboard. This makes it less messy when you start printing with the sponge.

2. Use a pencil to draw the outline of a ghost on the cardboard. Then, cut around the ghost, through the cardboard and the sponge.

3. Brush orange and yellow paint over a large piece of white paper. While it dries, draw a castle on blue paper. Cut it out and glue it on.

4. Lay some paper towels on an old newspaper. Then, spread white paint on the paper towels using the back of an old spoon.

5. Dip the sponge in the paint, then press it onto the castle. Rub the back slightly, then lift off the sponge. Print another ghost in the same way.

6. Follow steps 1-2 to make other ghosts and print them on the castle, too. When the paint is dry, add faces with a black felt-tip pen.

Dinosaur painting

Make the nose look like a beak.

1. Use a pencil to draw a dinosaur's nose, then add a line for the bottom jaw. Add a frill at the back of the head, then draw eyes and eyebrows.

2. Draw a fat body shape and a pointed tail. Then, add three short legs below the body – the fourth one is hidden.

3. Brush clean water over your drawing. Then, dab watery paint onto the water so that it runs. Dab more paint on the tummy and tail.

4. When the paint is dry, draw over the pencil lines with a black felt-tip pen. Add spots on the frill and toenails on the feet.

5. Using a red chalk pastel, draw lines on the dinosaur's body, tail and legs. Then, add a balloon and gift with a pencil.

6. Fill in the balloon and gift with watery paints. When they are dry, outline them with a black pen. Then, add more dinosaurs.

Princess collage

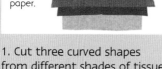

Glue them near the bottom of the paper.

Make the bodice overlap the skirt a little.

1. Cut three curved shapes from different shades of tissue paper, for the layers of the skirt. Glue them all onto a piece of paper, like this.

2. Cut a rectangle for the bodice of the dress and glue it on. Add two triangles for sleeves, then cut out circles and glue them on top.

3. Use a thin black felt-tip pen to draw two short lines for her neck. Add a curve for her face, then draw lots of wavy lines for her hair.

4. Draw around the top layer of the skirt, then draw along the sides and bottom of the other two layers. Add hands, and frills on her sleeves.

5. Draw eyes and a mouth. Use a red pencil to draw her cheeks and a line for her nose. Then, fill in her hair with a yellow pencil.

6. Draw a crown with a gold pen. Then, decorate her skirt, sleeves and body with patterns drawn with black and gold pens.

51

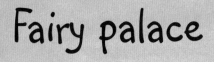

Fairy palace

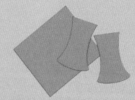

1. Pressing lightly with a pencil, draw some rounded hills on a piece of paper. Then, paint the hills in different shades of green.

2. For the palace, cut a square and two towers from bright paper. Make them small enough to fit onto one of the hills.

3. Paint a pale pink sky and a yellow sun. Then, glue the palace onto a hill. Cut roofs from pink paper and glue them onto the palace.

4. Cut out windows and doors from paper, then glue them onto the palace. Draw frames on them using a gold or silver pen.

5. Cut out some small paper hearts and glue them onto the top of each roof. Then, paint a few trees on the hills in the background.

6. Cut out photographs of flowers from magazines and glue them onto the background. Add stalks and leaves with pencils or pens.

Heart garland

1. Cut a long, thin strip of green paper. Then, fold it in half, with the short ends together, like this. Crease the fold really well.

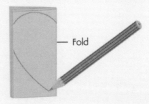

Fold

2. Fold the paper in half two more times. Then, draw half a heart on the folded paper, against the fold. Make the heart touch both edges.

Don't cut this part.

3. Draw a second line inside the first one. Then, holding all the layers together, carefully cut along both of the lines.

Flatten the garland.

4. Open out the garland and lay it on an old newspaper. Then, mix some paint and white glue together on an old plate.

5. Paint stripes on one of the hearts. Sprinkle glitter over the wet paint. Then, paint around another heart and sprinkle it with glitter.

6. Shake any excess glitter onto the newspaper. Glue sequins or paper shapes onto the other hearts, then leave the garland to dry.

55

Flower wall hanging

1. Lay a piece of plastic foodwrap on a magazine. Rip two shades of pink tissue paper into pieces.

2. Lay the pieces of tissue paper all over the foodwrap. Overlap them a little, like this.

3. Mix some white glue with water so that it is runny. Then, brush it over the tissue paper.

4. Add two more layers of tissue paper and glue. Then, sprinkle glitter on the top.

5. When the glue is dry, brush another layer of white glue over the glitter. Then, leave it to dry.

6. On another piece of plastic foodwrap, repeat steps 1-5, using yellow and orange tissue paper.

7. When it is dry, peel off the tissue paper. Cut out pink and orange flowers and small circles.

8. Glue pink circles onto the orange flowers and orange circles onto the pink flowers, like this.

9. Cut some pieces of thin ribbon. Then, tape the flowers onto them to make a wall hanging.

Octopus mobile

The slits should reach halfway.

1. Draw a four-legged octopus on cardboard. Cut it out, then draw around it on another piece of cardboard.

2. Cut out the other octopus. Hold them together, with one upside down. Cut a slit into both bodies.

3. Lay the bodies on a newspaper. Paint both sides with orange paint, then let the paint dry.

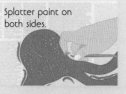

Splatter paint on both sides.

4. Dip a dry brush into blue paint. Then, flick the bristles to splatter paint over the bodies.

5. Draw lots of fish to hang from the mobile on another piece of cardboard. Cut out the shapes.

6. Cut eight long pieces of thread. Tape the fish onto the threads with sticky tape.

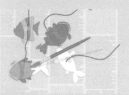

7. Paint both sides of the fish, then let the paint dry completely. Add faces with a black felt-tip pen.

8. Tape a thread onto each leg. Paint blue rings at the bottom for suckers. Then, let the paint dry.

9. Slot the slit of one body into the other. Draw a face. Open the mobile and add a thread for hanging.

Marzipan toadstools

To make 8 toadstools, you will need:
a block of 'white' marzipan*
red food dye

The toadstools need to be stored in
an airtight container and eaten
within three weeks.

*Marzipan contains ground nuts,
so don't give the toadstools to
anyone who is allergic to nuts.

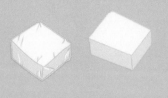

1. Unwrap the block of marzipan and cut it in half. Then, wrap one half in plastic foodwrap and put the other half in a small bowl.

2. Add three drops of red food dye to the bowl and mix it in with your fingers. Then, break the marzipan into eight pieces.

Wash your hands first.

3. Roll each piece into a ball, then squash them to make toadstool shapes. Press your thumb into the bottom to make a hollow, like this.

4. Unwrap the other half of the marzipan. To make spots, break off a third of the marzipan and roll it into lots of little balls.

5. Gently press several of the little balls onto each toadstool. Then, break the remaining piece of marzipan into eight pieces.

6. Roll each piece between your fingers to make a thick stalk. Then, press a red top onto each stalk to complete the toadstool.

Pastel butterflies

Draw right up to the fold.

1. Fold a piece of paper in half, then open it out. Using a black oil pastel, draw half a butterfly on one side.

2. Fold the paper in half again, then rub firmly over one side with the handle of a pair of scissors.

3. Unfold the paper. Then, use the pastel to draw over the faint outline of the other half of the butterfly.

4. Draw leaves around the butterfly. Then, paint the butterfly and leaves with bright inks or paints.

Paper flowers

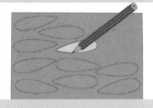

1. For the middles of the flowers, cut three cardboard cups from an egg carton. Paint them orange, then leave them to dry.

2. Draw a petal on thin cardboard and cut it out. Then, draw around it lots of times on bright paper and cut out the shapes.

3. Turn the orange cups over and glue the petals onto them, overlapping the petals a little. Then, leave the glue to dry.

4. Scrunch up three pieces of yellow tissue paper. Glue them into the middle of the orange cups, then let the glue dry.

5. For the stalks, press a piece of poster tack onto the back of each flower. Then, press a straw into the poster tack, like this.

Giraffe collage

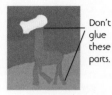

Don't glue these parts.

1. Glue brown paper onto cardboard. Rip another piece of paper, then glue it on the bottom.

2. Cut out a giraffe's body and legs. Cut a head from thick cardboard. Glue on all the pieces.

3. Rip brown paper patches and glue them onto the body. Add matchsticks around them.

4. Glue feathers or pieces of thread down the neck for the mane. Add long feathers on top.

5. Wrap black thread around each hoof and glue on feathers, matchsticks and pieces of shiny paper.

6. For antlers, glue a dried bean or seed onto each half of a wooden peg. Glue them onto the head.

7. Glue on feathers, with buttons on top, for the eyes. Then, glue down the rest of the head and legs.

8. For a bird, rip a paper body and wing. Join them with a paper fastener, then add a beak and claws.

Painted parrot

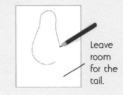

Leave room for the tail.

Leave the eye white.

1. Using a pencil, draw a shape for the parrot's head and body on a large piece of paper.

2. Draw an eye and a beak. Add some feathers on the head. Then, draw a branch and feet.

3. Fill in the beak and feet with yellow paint. Let the paint dry. Then, fill in the rest with red paint.

Use your right hand.

Print this wing first.

4. Paint a red tail, then leave it to dry. Add yellow feathers on top, then add green feathers.

5. On an old plate, spread red, yellow, green and blue paint in stripes. Press one hand into the paint.

6. Turn the paper upside down. Then, print a wing onto the body with your hand, like this.

7. Turn the plate so that the red paint is on the right. Print the other wing with your left hand.

8. Paint a black dot on the eye and leave it to dry. Then, fill in the branch with thick, brown paint.

Printed kings

1. Use a ballpoint pen to draw a simple picture of a king on a piece of thick cardboard.

2. Paint over the cardboard with a thick layer of white glue. Then, wash your brush.

3. Cut pieces of a thick rubber band to fit the main shapes. Then, press them on firmly.

4. Cut pieces of a narrower rubber band for the details. Press them onto the glue, too.

5. Cut lots of squares from a thick rubber band. Press them onto the background.

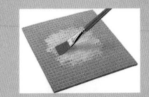

6. When the glue is completely dry, paint some thick paint onto a sponge cloth.

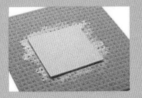

7. Lay the cardboard on the paint, with the picture facing down. Then, press firmly on the back.

8. Carefully lift the cardboard off the paper towels. Then, lay it face-up on an old newspaper.

9. Lay a piece of thin paper on the cardboard. Press the back of the paper firmly, then lift it off.

Cut-paper star card

1. Cut a rectangle and two smaller rectangles from paper or thin cardboard. Use a different shade of paper for each rectangle.

2. For the card itself, cut a rectangle of paper and fold it in half. Then, glue the largest rectangle on top and trim the edges.

3. Glue the smallest rectangle of paper onto the back of a piece of shiny paper or giftwrap. Then, trim around it.

4. Using a craft knife, carefully cut several lines that cross each other near the top of the paper. Then, push a pencil through the cuts.

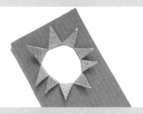

5. Gently fold each triangle back. Crease the folds well, so that the shiny paper makes a star shape on the front of the paper, like this.

6. Glue both paper rectangles onto the card, with the small one on top. Draw a pattern in the star with gold pen, then glue on gold paper shapes.

Rain fairy

1. Use a pencil to draw a circle for the fairy's head. Then, add a dress with a wavy bottom edge. Draw her arms, legs and wings, too.

2. Draw her hair, eyes and eyelashes, nose and a big smile. Then, draw heart-shaped lips on the smile. Add a wand in her hand.

The wax resists the paint.

3. Use a white wax crayon to draw lines for raindrops around the fairy. They are shown in yellow here so that you can see them.

4. Brush water over the paper. Then, brush watery pink paint on top so that it spreads. Add some blobs of yellow paint, too.

5. When the paint is dry, draw over all your pencil lines with different felt-tip pens. Add patterns on the fairy's dress, too.

6. Dip a thin paintbrush into water, then brush it over the pen lines so that the ink runs. Rinse your brush after you do each part of the fairy.

Prisoner trick

For this trick, you will need:
A piece of paper
A pair of scissors
A pencil
A glue stick
String

1. Using scissors, cut out two rectangles of paper, about the size of a playing card. Make them exactly the same size.

2. Draw lines that look like prison bars on one piece of paper, using a pencil. Then, draw a prisoner on the other piece.

3. Spread glue over the back of the paper with lines on it. Cut a piece of string, then lay it across the middle of the paper, like this.

4. Press the other piece of paper on top, with the prisoner facing up. Make sure that all the edges line up. Then, leave the glue to dry.

5. Show the audience both sides of the card. Tell them that the man is an escaped prisoner and you are going to recapture him.

6. Hold the ends of the string, so that the prisoner is upside down, facing you. Then, spin the card quickly between your fingers and thumbs.

Shimmering shapes

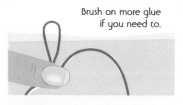

Brush on more glue
if you need to.

1. Use a pencil to draw a heart on a piece of tissue paper. Lay it on some plastic foodwrap, then brush white glue along the pencil line.

2. Press a length of thread onto the glue. At the top of the heart, make a loop with the thread and press the end into the glue.

3. Brush a thin layer of glue inside the heart. Then, cut some pieces of thread and press them into the glue, so that they overlap.

4. Brush another layer of glue over the top. Lightly sprinkle glitter over the shape and leave it until the glue has completely dried.

5. Carefully peel the tissue paper off the foodwrap and cut around the heart. Then, glue some sequins between the threads.

Sea horse pencil top

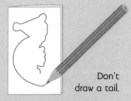

Don't
draw a tail.

1. Fold a piece of thick paper
in half. Draw a sea horse's
body, like this. Then, cut out
the shape, through both
layers of paper.

This will
be the tail.

2. Bend a pipe cleaner into
a curved shape that follows
the sea horse's body. Lay it
on the sea horse and tape
it in place.

Squeeze the
edges until the
glue dries.

3. Spread white glue over the
paper and the pipe cleaner.
Then, press the other sea
horse on top and squeeze
the edges together.

4. When the glue is dry, paint
both sides of the sea horse's
body. Paint along the edges
of the body, then paint the
pipe cleaner, too.

5. When the paint is dry,
paint patterns and an eye
on each side of the sea
horse. Then, wind the tail
around the end of a pencil.

Curl the tail into
a spiral for a
sea horse
charm.

81

Tissue paper birds

1. Rip a rough shape for a bird's body from pink tissue paper. Then, rip two shapes for the wings and another for the tail.

Brush the glue to the edge.

2. Gently brush white glue on the back of the body. Press it onto a piece of white paper, then glue on the wings and tail.

3. Rip a shape for another bird's body and two shapes for wings from blue tissue paper. Then, glue them onto the paper, too.

4. Rip lots of small pieces from pink tissue paper. Glue them in the spaces around the birds, then leave the glue to dry.

5. Using a black felt-tip pen, draw outlines for the birds' bodies. You don't need to follow the edges of the tissue paper too closely.

6. Draw the birds' tails, wings, legs and beaks. Add eyes and feathers on their heads. Draw hearts on the small pieces of tissue paper.

City painting

1. Cut a large rectangle of grey paper, then fold it in half with its long sides together. Crease the fold, then open the paper.

2. Use a white oil pastel to draw a thick line above the fold. Draw lots of buildings, trees, street lights, a moon and stars.

3. Fold the paper again, then rub all over it with the back of a spoon. This will transfer a copy of your pastel drawing onto the other half.

4. Open the paper. Then, paint the top half of the picture with dark blue ink or watery paint. The pastel will resist the paint.

5. Mix the ink or paint with water to make it more watery. Paint below the fold, then brush darker lines on top to make it look like water.

6. When the ink or paint is dry, draw over the moon and lights with a yellow pastel. Fold the paper and rub over it to make reflections.

Princess bookmark

1. Draw the outline of a tower on a piece of blue cardboard. Make the tower wider at the top than at the bottom. Then, cut it out.

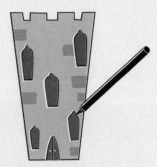

2. Using blue paint, add bricks on the tower. Add darker blue windows and a door, too. Then, outline them with a thin black pen.

Use a black pen.

3. Draw the top half of a princess on a piece of cardboard. Fill her in with paints, then leave her to dry. Add outlines and a face.

4. Use scissors to cut out the princess. Slot her hair over the top of the tower. Then, tape her body to the back of the tower.

Scratched patterns

1. Use different oil pastels to draw lots of patches on a piece of white paper. Make sure that the patches join together, like this.

2. Mix a little water with some thick black paint. Use acrylic paint if you have it. Cover the oil pastel patches completely with the paint.

3. Leave the paint until it is almost dry. Then, use a screwdriver to gently scratch lines in the paint, to reveal the oil pastels underneath.

4. Scratch several more lines down the paint. Then, scratch lines across it to make a large grid. Scratch a border, too.

5. Scratch a simple outline of a bird in part of the grid. Then, add some curved lines for feathers, a wing, an eye and a beak.

6. If you make a mistake, paint over it with some black paint. Let the paint dry a little before you scratch into it again.

Rainy sky picture

1. Wet some thick, absorbent paper with clean water. Then, mix dark blue watery paint with brown to make dark grey.

2. Paint overlapping stripes of dark grey across the top of the paper. They don't need to be even or to start in the same place.

3. While the grey paint is wet, add blue stripes across the middle of the paper. Then, add grey ones at the bottom, like this.

4. Before the paint has dried, wipe a tissue across the paint so that the bottom is almost white. Then, leave it to dry.

5. For the tree, dab a blob of grey paint near the bottom of the paper. Add a green trunk and dashes for grass, using a thin paintbrush.

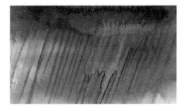

6. When the painting is dry, use a thin brush to paint fine grey lines for rain, coming from the dark area near the top of the picture.

Sparkly wand

1. Draw a star for a template on a piece of cardboard. Cut it out, then lay it on another piece of cardboard and draw

2. Cut out the stars and paint them on one side. Then, cut 10 pieces of thin ribbon that are half as long as a drinking straw.

3. Lay one of the stars on a piece of scrap paper. Then, spread white glue over the side that has not been painted, like this.

4. Carefully lay the straw and the pieces of ribbon on top of the glue, like this. Then, spread glue on the other star and lay it on top.

The paper protects the book.

5. Lay a sheet of paper over the star. Then, put a heavy book on top, and leave the wand for an hour, until the glue is completely dry.

6. Glue lots of sequins, glitter and tiny beads onto one side of the wand. Wait for the glue to dry, then decorate the other side, too.

Cut-and-stick girl

1. Cut pieces of paper with patterns on them from old magazines. Cut out pictures of hair, ears and lips, too.

2. Cut out a hairstyle shape from a photograph in a magazine. Glue it onto a piece of white paper.

3. Lay tracing paper over the hair and draw a face and neck. Turn the paper over and rub a pencil over the lines.

4. Turn the tracing paper back over. Lay it on paper with a skin tone. Draw over the face again, then cut it out.

5. Glue on the face, then glue on a mouth and ear, too. Draw eyes and a nose. Then, add a patterned paper dress.

Add a teddy bear, too.

6. Cut out legs, arms and a pair of shoes and glue them on. Add a short sleeve and a heart-shaped pocket, too.

Painted dinosaurs

1. For a dinosaur with a long neck, draw a large oval in the middle of your paper. Then, add two smaller ovals for the tops of the legs.

2. Draw a small oval for the head, above and to one side of the body. Draw a long curved neck, then add a very long tail.

3. Draw the two nearest legs coming down from the ovals you drew in step 1. Then, draw the other two legs beside them.

4. Draw over the outline and around the legs with a green pencil. Add an eye and a mouth. Then, erase all the other pencil lines.

5. Fill in the dinosaur with watery paint. While the paint is still wet, paint some darker blobs on the back, neck and tail. Let it dry.

You could paint other kinds of dinosaurs using the same method.

Mermaid chain

1. Fold a rectangle of paper in half, with its short sides together. Then, fold it in half again.

2. Draw a mermaid with her arms out, so that her hands almost touch the edges of the paper.

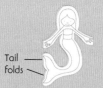

3. Draw the tail curving to one side, making the tips of the tail close to the edge of the paper.

4. Draw a line around the mermaid that touches the edges of the paper by the hands and tail.

Don't cut here.

5. Cut along the line above the mermaid's arms and head. Don't cut around her hands.

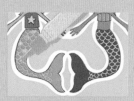

Tail folds

6. Cut along the lines around the arms and tail. Don't cut the folds by the tail and hands.

7. Unfold the paper. Draw mermaids in the other shapes and decorate them all with felt-tip pens.

8. Using a shiny pen, draw scales on the tails and patterns on the tops. Add dots of glitter glue, too.

Flowery boxes

1. Cut or rip lots of shapes from bright tissue paper. Then, spread white glue on them and press them all over a box.

2. Cut lots of pictures of different kinds of flowers from old magazines. Cut as close to the edges of the flowers as you can.

3. Brush white glue onto the back of one of the paper flowers. Then, place the flower on the top of the box, like this.

4. Gently rub the flower, to make it really flat. Then, glue another flower onto the box, a little way from the first one.

5. Glue on lots more flowers. Glue some of them so that they go over the edges of the box. Then, press them down.

The glue will be clear when it dries.

6. Brush a thick layer of white glue over the whole box, including the flowers. Then, leave the glue to dry completely.

Pirate door sign

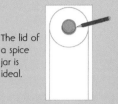

The lid of a spice jar is ideal.

1. Lay a roll of sticky tape near the top of a long piece of thick white paper. Then, draw around the sticky tape with a pencil.

2. Draw two lines from the circle to the bottom of the paper. Lay the lid of a small jar in the middle of the circle and draw around it.

3. Draw two curving lines from the small circle, like this. Then, cut out the door sign shape, following the pencil lines.

4. Draw a pirate's head halfway down the main part of the door sign. Add a headscarf, hair and ears, then draw his face.

5. Draw his body, arms and sword, then draw over all the lines with a black felt-tip pen. Then, fill in the picture with other pens.

6. Draw stripes across the sign and fill them in with a red pen. Then, write your name or a message on the pirate's sword, like this.

Cut-paper flowers

1. Draw around three differently sized round objects on different shades of thick paper.

2. Cut out the circles. Lay the middle-sized object in the big circle and draw around it.

3. Draw a line across the big circle. Add a second line, crossing it. Then, draw two more lines, like this.

4. Draw petals from the edge of the big circle to the edge of the middle circle. Cut around the petals.

5. Glue the small circle onto the middle-sized one. Make small cuts around the edge.

6. Glue the smaller circles onto the big one. Tape one end of a straw to the back of the flower.

7. Press a piece of poster tack onto the other end of the straw and press it into a jar.

8. Scrunch up lots of pieces of tissue paper and push them into the jar, around the stalk.

9. Cut two pointed leaves from green paper. Then, glue them onto the stalk, like this.

Painted patterns

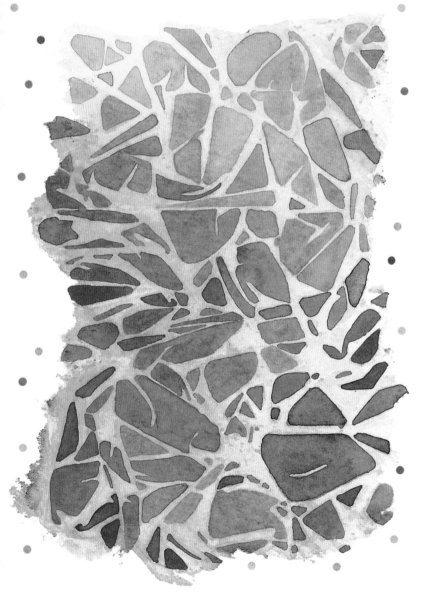

1. Mix some different shades of bright watery paint. Then, paint them in patches close to each other on a piece of white paper.

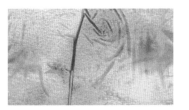

2. Before the paint has dried, cut a piece of plastic foodwrap that is larger than your painting. Then, lay it over the paint.

3. Using your fingers, move the paint around under the foodwrap. This blends the different shades together and makes patterns.

4. Leave the foodwrap on top of the paint and let the paint dry completely. Then, carefully peel the foodwrap off the paper.

5. Use watery paints to fill in lots of the patterns left by the foodwrap. Make sure you leave a space around each shape.

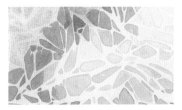

6. Fill in more of the patterns, using some strong shades of paint and some paler ones. Leave some of the patterns unfilled.

Index

Pages 52, 53, 100 & 101, Images of flowers © Digital Vision

Written by Fiona Watt, Rebecca Gilpin, Leonie Pratt, Anna Milbourne, Ruth Brocklehurst and Ben Denne.

Designed & illustrated by Antonia Miller, Josephine Thompson, Non Figg, Katrina Fearn, Katie Lovell,
Amanda Gulliver, Erica Harrison, Vici Leyhane, Jan McCafferty, Rachel Wells, Lucy Parris, Natacha Goransky,
Michelle Lawrence, Russell Punter, Molly Sage and Andi Good. Digital manipulation by Pete Taylor.